# How to Keep a Pet Squirrel

Illustrated by Axel Scheffler

**ff**

*faber and faber*

Text taken from *The Children's Encyclopedia*, 1910
Edited by Arthur Mee, The Educational Book Company Limited, London

First published in Germany in 2009
by Jacoby Stuart
First published in the UK in 2010
by Faber and Faber Limited
Bloomsbury House, 74–77 Great Russell Street,
London WC1B 3DA

Printed in the UK by Butler Tanner and Dennis Ltd

ISBN 978–0–571–25598–6

The squirrel is the monkey of our woods.

FRIEDRICH VON TSCHUDI

The squirrel makes a very attractive and interesting pet, but we should always see that the animal we obtain is a young one, and, if possible, a squirrel that is born in captivity.

It is unkind to capture an animal that leads so active and
unfettered a life,

after it has passed infancy and knows what the freedom
of the woods is like;

and, in any case, such an animal is difficult to tame,
and is always likely, when suddenly alarmed, to give our
finger a nasty nip with its teeth.

The squirrel born in captivity is almost invariably free
from this undesirable habit, and can be tamed much
more easily.

It is very cruel to keep such an animal in a small cage,

and above all to place it in one of those cages which
consists entirely, or almost entirely of a revolving wheel.

A roomy cage should be provided, in which a revolving
wheel is merely an apartment to which the squirrel can
resort or not as it likes.

In this form the wheel is useful, as it enables the squirrel to take the exercise without which it cannot keep healthy.

We must remember that the squirrel is by nature a very agile creature, springing about from tree to tree and playing among the leafy branches almost incessantly.

No cage should ever have its main compartment less than three feet square, and five feet high: and if we can provide a bigger one for our pet all the better.

Near the roof a sleeping box about a foot square should
be provided, and warmly lined with soft clean hay. The
floor must be sprinkled with sawdust, and this should
be covered over with hay or broken straw to prevent it
being scattered all over the cage as the squirrel scampers
over the box.

A tree branch should be firmly fixed in the cage, one
fork leading to the sleeping-box,

and in a large cage a trapeze may be added.

In buying a squirrel it is best to obtain our animal in
September, when its coat is in the best condition.

The feet must be clean,

the eyes bright, and the teeth white.

If the teeth are yellow the animal is old and should be rejected, for it will be difficult and perhaps impossible to tame it.

Kind and gentle care will soon make a young squirrel
very friendly and affectionate.

The feeding of a pet squirrel is by no means a difficult matter.

Plenty of nuts should be provided, beech, Barcelona, walnut, hazel, and monkey nuts, but not the oily kinds like the Brazil.

Acorns, wheat, and stale bread are all useful, and boiled rice, and bread-and-milk, well strained, should be given regularly.

Carrot, swede, apple, and boiled potato are also good,
and occasionally a little cooked meat.

Of course, if the animal is very young when we first get it we must break the shells of the nuts and chop up the kernels very small.

Later on it will learn to do this for itself, but it must be brought on to adult food gradually. Two meals a day are sufficient.

It is very necessary that the cage should be kept
thoroughly clean, and a supply of fresh water must be
provided all the time.

Squirrels are certainly very attractive pets,

and we shall never tire of watching their playful tricks,

graceful actions

and queer attitudes.

But they can be strong-willed.

# On the Squirrel

Taken from Conrad Gesner's *Allgemeines Thier-Buch (Universal Animal Book)*, 1669

The squirrel is a nimble and restless little beast. Tho' passably wild by nature, it can nevertheless grow so tame that it will frolic in bodices and sleeves, scamper about a master or mistress's head and hide itself in a person's dress . . .

When a squirrel out looking for food comes upon a river that it would cross, it finds itself a chip of wood, seats itself upon it, hoists its tail in place of a sail, trims this appendage to the wind and so navigates the channel. They have been sighted crossing rivers in this fashion carrying a pine- or fir-cone lodged between their teeth.

If the summer sun gives off too fierce a heat, a squirrel will use its tail as an awning and by this means furnish itself with shade.

Save Our Squirrels

When the text for this book was first written in 1910, grey squirrels were still something of a novelty and it was our beautiful native red squirrel that people commonly saw in the parks and gardens of Britain. In that era, having a tame red squirrel (or a dormouse or water vole) was seen to be part and parcel of helping a child to learn about and respect nature. However, 100 hundred years on, although there are around 150,000 red squirrels left in Britain, only 25,000 remain on mainland England. In contrast, it is estimated that the UK hosts over 4 million grey squirrels!

Save our Squirrels is there to protect England's remaining red squirrels in their stronghold Northern counties, working with institutions and volunteers to help ensure our children and grandchildren still have a chance to see this adorable mammal in the wild rather than in a cage. By buying this book, you have already helped make a difference, but if you would like more information about red squirrels and the threats they face, or how you can help save them too, visit our website:

www.saveoursquirrels.org